Contents

The Aroma *After the* Rain

33 Days of Inspirational Messages for Women

Linda M. Beltran

ISBN 979-8-89130-245-7 (paperback)
ISBN 979-8-89130-246-4 (digital)

Christian Faith Publishing
832 Park Avenue
Meadville, PA 16335
www.christianfaithpublishing.com

Printed in the United States of America

Introduction

These written expressions of inspiring words are for individuals all around the world. These are brimming with reminders from God's Word to all of us that he is always with us as we walk through the valleys of uncertainty and sit atop the peaceful mountain.

The Aroma After the Rain was written to help you gain greater insight into how much God truly loves you. He desires for you to have the best quality of life that goes beyond your own understanding.

This can begin by starting your day with God's inspirational words for you by spending a few minutes of your time to sit and hear what he will speak to you for your soul to be uplifted.

In this book, I have inserted scriptures with messages to help you be encouraged, strengthened, challenged, and refreshed by inspirational words as well as God's personal word to you.

Embrace every word spoken to you and seek a closer relationship with Jesus.
Believe and Receive!

I Will Answer You

*Call to Me, and I will answer you and show you
great and mighty things, which you do not know.*

Jeremiah 33:3 NKJV

Many times, in life, we question where God is because we see don't see anything happening. His timing is perfect, and he keeps his promises to us. He is not man such that he would lie. He may not always provide the answer when you want it, but he is always on time. God's request to us is to simply trust, believe, be patient, and always call on him; that he be your first resort instead of the last.

He is your healer, lawyer, counselor, peacemaker, problem solver, and much more.

God is always working behind the scenes on the solution to our problems. But are we willing to do what he instructs us to do to attain it? That is the question for us. Listen to his gentle and quiet whisper in everything that we do. Spending time alone with God is the best way to develop our eyesight and hearing—our eyesight for seeing what he is doing around us and our hearing for listening to his instruction.

*****

Lord, help us hear your voice so clearly that we have no doubt that we are hearing you and following your instructions about any circumstance or situation before us.

For insight: Proverbs 3:5–6 NIV,
Psalm 37:5 NLT.

Believe to Receive

Therefore, I tell you, whatever you ask for in prayer, believe that you have received it, and it will be yours.

Mark 11:24 NIV

We may find it difficult to believe for ourselves at times that we can receive blessings or that our prayers are even being answered. We get discouraged because we see others around us receiving their blessings and getting their prayers answered more quickly than us, and then we begin to think that God has forgotten us. This is far from the truth. Some prayers arrive sooner than we think, and others will take more time. But we must wait patiently, knowing that they will all come in God's time, not ours. Don't allow your mind to be unsettled or disturbed when you are not seeing things come to pass as quickly as you would want them to. His plans for you have been

set in motion; don't focus on the distractions that eas-
ily draw you away from what is before you and what
is to come. We must constantly remind ourselves of
whose report and word will we believe.

*****

Lord, we ask that you help us to not waver from
what we know is true: that you keep your Word to
us all.

For insight: Matthew 21:22 NKJV,
Mark 9:23 NLT.

You Are My Strength

*The Lord is my strength and my shield; my
heart trusts in him and he helps me.*

Psalm 28:7 NIV

We need to ask for the Lord's strength to endure life's trials with joy. When we face challenges in our lives, our faith is tested and it teaches us not to rely on ourselves to solve our problems. When we go through situations in life, we gain compassion for other people who may be going through similar difficulties that we have already gone through, and then we may in some way be able to help them along the way. The joy of the Lord enables us to enjoy our journey through life, whether we are in good or bad circumstances. Joy is our strength and a weapon that we use in spiritual warfare. If we are constantly complaining, we are giving our joy away a little at a time until we have nothing left. When our joy is gone, we stay stuck in a situation and are not able to move forward because of it. We must not lose our joy in the midst of difficulties because true joy comes from the Lord who provides us with the strength we need to keep moving forward.

*****

Lord, help us to not give away our joy when we go through hard times. We ask for your help to stay steadfast and unmovable with and through your strength.

For insight: Philippians 4:13 ESV,
Psalm 27:1 KJV.

Seek Him

*You will seek me and find me when
you seek me with all your heart.*

Jeremiah 29:13 NIV

God's Word renews our mind and brings clarity, direction, and instruction in matters affecting our lives. We need to get engrafted in his Word to find the hidden mysteries that he says we should seek in order to find them. They will be revealed to those who seek them in his Word, readings, and teachings. The Lord has shown us many things to teach us how to go beyond the normal and into the realm of the supernatural, where he dwells. Are we wanting to know more about God? If so, we need to put ourselves aside and seek him. He wants to take us to a higher level, where we are wanting more of him and less of our fleshly desires so that we can see beyond the natural. We must see the miraculous works of God and how we can also walk in that authority. The Lord wants us to walk in the Spirit and worship him freely with our hearts open to receive the new things that he has for us.

*****

Lord, we ask that you help us seek you with all our hearts so that we may see your wonderous works in all that is around us.

For insight: Matthew 6:33 NIV,
1 Chronicles 16:11 NIV.

His Direction

*This is what the Lord says your Redeemer,
the Holy One of Israel: I am the Lord your
God, who teaches you what is best for you,
who directs you in the way you should go.*

Isaiah 48:17 NIV

The Lord is the director of the paths in our lives if we allow him, and he will give us divine instructions. We need to acknowledge who he is and that we need his guidance in all areas of our lives. The Lord delights in helping us because he desires for us to trust and seek his face in all matters for direction. He will instruct and teach us the way we should go when we ask for his help when we need direction in what concerns us. We need to want to hear his voice so that we would know which way to go or what to do. Our part is to set aside time daily to pray and commune with God so that we can hear what he has to say in the matters we bring before him and then be confident that he does hear our prayers and will answer them in time.

*****

Lord, we ask that you direct our path—that we may know the way we should go, what we can do, and when we should act in matters that come our way in life.

For insight: Philippians 4:6 NIV,
Psalm 25:5 NKJV.

You Are Chosen

If you belonged to the world, it would love you as its own. As it is, you do not belong to the world, but I have chosen you out of the world.

John 15:19 NIV

The Lord chose us before the formation of the world, and he wove us in our mother's womb. We were created by the Master's Hand and designed to be unique, and he has called us out by name. We have been hand-picked by God from others. He calls many, but only a few answer and respond to his drawing, and there are others who do not receive him into their lives. The Lord gives us free will to accept or reject him. We are never forced to do anything; it is entirely up to us. He has good plans for us and wants to use all of us to touch others by sharing what he has done in our own personal lives, which is called a testimony. We all have a plan that has been set out especially for us individually, that only we can fulfill, and it is called destiny. We can only do this by following the path that he has laid out before us.

*****

We are indebted to you, Lord, for drawing us to you, and we are very grateful because you kept pursuing us. For the great love you have for us, we are grateful as well.

For insight: Matthew 22:14 NIV,
1 Peter 2:9 NKJV.

His Word Will Keep You

*For I know the plans I have for you," declares
the L*ORD*, plans to prosper you and not to harm
you, plans to give You hope and a future.*

Jeremiah 29: 11 NIV

When the winds of life blow, his Word will keep you and sustain you just as palm trees bend back and forth to the point of touching the ground without breaking under the pressure. When we face storms in our lives and it feels like we are at the point of breaking, God sends his fresh wind to blow upon us and help us remain steadfast and unmovable. He is the source of our strength; all we need to do is call upon him in times of trouble, and he will see us through it all. The strength and flexibility of the palm tree should be an inspiration to us all in withstanding the storms of life with God and, at the end, continue standing in the midst of it all.

*****

Lord, help us keep growing our roots deep in your Word, your truth, and your everlasting love.

For insight: Psalm 92:12 NIV,
Exodus 15:13 NLV.

God's Best for You

In Him also we have obtained an inheritance, being predestined according to the purpose of Him who works all things according to the counsel of His will.

Ephesians 1:11 NKJV

The Lord is always wanting us to have the best for our lives, and most of the time, we settle for less because that's all we think we deserve. We impose our own limits on our lives, which are usually lower than what God has in store for us. We get stuck in a poverty mentality because we have had a lack in many areas of our lives growing up. We believe that will always be the case, and this is what keeps us from receiving God's best. That's where the root begins. We need to change our way of thinking and remind ourselves about what God says to us in his Word—those are his promises for us. We are to look up and claim what he has in store for us: good health, prosperity, and so on. It is all there within our reach if we just grab a hold of it for ourselves and expect to receive it.

*****

We are honored, Lord, because you desire to give us your best, which you place within our grasp. It is beyond our own imagination.

For insight: Joshua 1:8 NIV,
Philippians 4:8 NIV.

Follow His Lead

*I will instruct you and teach you in the way
you should go; I will guide you with My eye.*

Psalm 32: 8 NKJV

As we are all aware, the Lord lets us know that our way of thinking and doing things are not his. We need to be sensitive to God's promptings and do what he is asking us to do, then we will know we are doing things his way by the peace we have. There will be times we might not see what is up ahead, but the Lord will give us small hints that we need to pay attention to along the way. When the Lord has asked us to do something, we should never back down from it just because it might get hard. Sometimes he will lead us along that hard way instead of the easy way because he is working in us. How else would we learn to lean on him for direction for everything

in our lives if it is easy and we can handle it by ourselves? If that is the case, we would lean on our own
understanding and not on his. In all things, we are to
ask the Lord for direction in our plans, job seeking,
and so on. As we ask for the Lord's direction and
guidance in all decision-making, he will lead us in
the way we should go.

*****

Thank you, Lord, for whenever we allow you to
be our GPS (God's Personal Service), you are always
willing and able to direct us.

For insight: Isaiah 30:21 NIV,
Jeremiah 33:3 NIV.

Not Hearing God

He who has ears to hear, let them hear!

Matthew 11:15 NKJV

There are times in our lives that we stop hearing God's voice because we have put him on mute, and we procrastinate doing what needs to be done on our part to be able to hear him once again. There are windows of opportunity around us that we may be missing because our ears are closed to his voice. We need to ask ourselves, "What is keeping us from hearing his voice? Are we being distracted, and if so, what are those things that we have put before him?" We must ask these questions so that we can get these distractions out of our lives to be able to hear again. We need to ask the Lord to fix our hearing so that we can listen to what he is saying to us specifically. We always need to plug into the source, which is God himself, and ask him, "What are you saying to me, Lord, that I am not hearing?" We must tune in to God to clearly hear what he is saying, and we must stop sending his calls to voicemail.

*****

Lord, we ask that you give us ears to hear when you are speaking to us.

For insight: Hebrews 2:1 NIV,
Isaiah 30:21 NIV.

Open Your Heart

*My son, give me your heart and let
your eyes delight in my ways.*

Psalm 23:26 NIV

We all seek something that will fill the empty spot in our hearts that we can never seem to fill. There is only one who can fill it, and that is God alone. That space has only been reserved for him. We try to fill our lives with materialistic things and relationships, thinking that this will fill our hearts, but we still feel empty. If we simply open our hearts to the Lord, who is gently knocking on the door, we will see that he is all we need to fill that emptiness. God will never force himself on us. He will always ask for our permission to enter because he has given us free will to answer or ignore the knock.

*****

Lord, we thank you for standing at the door of my heart. Even now, we ask you to enter our hearts and fill them completely.

For insight: Proverbs 4:23 NLV,
Psalm 37:4 NIV.

Meditate on the Word

But his delight is in the law of the Lord; and in His law doth he meditates day and night.

Psalm 1:2 NKJV

It is beneficial to us all to spend quality time reading God's Word. Just as we make time for other things, we should make reading God's Word a priority in our lives. The more we spend time meditating on his Word, the more we will reap from it, which also helps strengthen our inner being. In reading, we will receive revelation, virtue, knowledge, and much more. We will get much more insight from the Word the more time we spend time studying it. Our minds need to be renewed day by day, and it is vital that we read and press onward to gain the wisdom that has been written for our benefit and growth. Before beginning to read, we must pray to quiet our minds so that we will not miss what the Lord is attempting to say and reveal to us. It is also important to stop and think every once in a while to remove any distractions from our minds. That way, we can give our full attention to his Word.

*****

Lord, help us quiet our minds so that we may receive all that you have for us in your written word.

For insight: Joshua 1:8 NIV,
Job 22:22 NIV.

Give It Your Best Shot

Fight the good fight of the faith. Take hold of eternal life to which you were called when you made your good confession in the presence of many witnesses.

1 Timothy 6:12 NIV

Many times, we ask ourselves, "Why am I going through these difficult situations?" instead of, "How will this be beneficial to my life?" The thing is, we expect everything to be easy. And as we have seen through life's experiences, we find that is anything but true. How else will the Lord prepare us for life's trials if not through the afflictions that come our way? Similarly, wrestlers and boxers must go through hard and difficult training to build up their muscle and stamina. They also need to make it a daily part of their lives. We also are training so that we may be able to withstand the punches thrown at us by life. We must endure, persevere, and then become strengthened spiritually, mentally, and physically. This will help us to endure all the discomfort while becoming even stronger.

*****

Lord, you are our strength. Help us fight victoriously until our last breath has gone.

For insight: 2 Timothy 4:7 NIV,
1 Thessalonians 5:16–18 NIV.

Speak What God Says about You

*Therefore, if anyone is in Christ, he is a
new creation; Old things have passed away;
behold all things have become new.*

2 Corinthians 5:17 NKJV

We need to pay attention to what we say about ourselves. Whatever we speak, our spirit hears, and then you believe what you say about yourself. There is power in the words that come out of our mouths. We will either lift ourselves up or tear ourselves down with our own words. You may say that you are unlovable, weak, broken, rejected, and purposeless. But God says that you are his beloved; he makes you strong. He has made you whole. You are his, and God has created you with a purpose and much more.

Believe God's Word instead of what you feel. Let's think before we speak, and say what God says about you because his Word to us is an abundant life. Keep your head up high because of who you belong to.

*****

Lord, we ask you to remind us to speak words that will bring life to ourselves instead of destruction.

For insight: Psalm 139: 14–17 NIV,
Revelation 2:17 NLV

Speak the Word

In the beginning was the Word, and the Word was with God, and the Word was God.

John 1:1 NIV

The Word, who entered the world as a defense-less infant, was the same one who created our world and brought it into being. All things were spoken into existence by every word that proceeded out of the mouth of God. As heirs of the kingdom, we have been given the same authority to speak life or death into our own lives just as God spoke the world into existence. We are to speak over our lives and the lives of our family, children, grandchildren, and friends. We are to speak good health, prosperity, and blessings beyond measure over them all. As we speak good things over our lives, those words are like seeds being planted in good soil. They begin to take root and grow so that we may reap the benefits as we go through life.

*****

Lord, help us speak good things over our lives so that we can reap the good seeds we have sown throughout time.

For insight: Isaiah 55:11 NIV,
Proverbs 18:21 ESV.

Know His Voice

My sheep listen to my voice; I know them, and they follow me.

John 10:27 NIV

God's Word speaks about how the Lord is our shepherd and we are the sheep and how we are to follow him. We must understand God's character and nature by staying in his Word and continually spending intimate time with him. The more we study, the better we will be able to hear, discern, and obey his direction. We can recognize God's still, small voice and his guidance in our lives by knowing his voice through the Scripture. The Lord gives us discernment to be able to identify the difference between the distinctive voice of God and the voices of deception. We often fall into the trap of believing deceptive voices because they lead us to believe that something false is the truth. The Lord is constantly speaking to us and wants to give us direction in all things, but most of the time, we are not listening to his voice of truth.

*****

Thank you, Lord, for giving us insight to recognize the false voices that try to lead us away from you and for opening our ears to hear your precious voice.

For insight: Psalm 23 NIV,
Revelation 3:20 NKJV.

You Are Unique to God

For you created my inmost being; you knit me together in my mother's womb.

Psalm 139: 13 NIV

You were born to shine; you are priceless. Be who God wants you to be. We may think of ourselves as small, cowardly, or unable. You are called and equipped; he has given you power and authority, and you are designed to live an abundant life. God has given you gifts and talents to use and share with others around you. Before we are called to do something great, we are shown how special we are and how valuable we are to God. What God has for you, no one else has. He has a special plan just for you. Be after God's heart, and you will be led to the bridges that he will have you cross because destiny awaits you. He is setting you up for greatness; are you ready when he says go? We can know God's calling by being obedient to what he told us last.

*****

Lord, help us follow your lead as you have directed us by speaking to us individually so that we may arrive at our destination.

For insight: Ephesians 2:10 NIV,
1 Corinthians 7:17 NIV.

He Is My Song

*And he hath put a new song in my
mouth, even praise unto our God.*

Psalm 40:3 KJV

Singing has a way of bringing your heart, soul, and mind together so that it helps you focus entirely on the Lord and not on the challenges we may be going through in our lives. The hard times can make us bitter or better, but when we keep a song in our hearts and sing it out loud, we stay focused on the things above instead of the things around us. In the midst of the rains when they come, it is very important to sing our song to the Lord because it uplifts our spirit. When we sing, it comes forth like a spring from our mouths, and God inhabits the praise that flows before him. This also helps clear our minds off what is ahead of us and what we should do in whatever situation we are in at the time. Make your own song—one that you have never sung before—to the Lord about how good he has been to you and how through it all he has never failed you.

*****

Lord, we ask that when we sing our song unto you, it may spring up as a well to quench our spirit when we are feeling dry.

For insight: Psalm 98:1 NLT,
Numbers 21:17 NIV.

Keep the Vision

*God is able to make all grace abound toward you,
that you, always having all sufficiency in all things,
may have an abundance for every good work.*

Proverbs 29:18 NKJV

God wants to give us a deeper revelation of who he is, first of all, and then he will show us the plans he has in store for us. As we read his Word and spend time in prayer, that is when he will reveal to us dreams and visions that are far greater than we can ever imagine for ourselves. Nothing in the world can satisfy you like what God has in store for you. When the Lord reveals his plans to us for our lives, we are to write them down so that we can remind ourselves of what he has shown us and what we are needing to do to get there. Then we are to give it all we have and

go after it. The Lord will always equip us with what
we need in order to fulfill the vision he has given us.

*****

Lord, we ask that you remind us to look back
at the written vision that you gave us. We know you
will always provide the things we need to carry out
the call on our lives.

For insight: 2 Corinthians 9:8 NIV,
Habakkuk 2:2 NKJV.

Touch His Garment

And all the crowd sought to touch him, for power came out from him and healed them all.

Luke 6:19 ESV

God is our joy, peace, and strength. All we have to do is accept and allow him to be our comforter in times of need for healing of various kinds. The Lord waits for those of us who are burdened, down in heart, or physically sick to come to him, but we usually choose to keep him out of the picture. When we do that, we usually become anxious and lose our peace. We always take matters into our own hands, thinking that we can do better, but our ways are not God's ways. He would show us what he is able to do if we would just believe and not allow unbelief to override what we know he is able to do according to his Word. If we only allow him to heal us—the

Lord heals the brokenhearted in spirit and much more. God is able to heal the deaf so that they may hear and the mute so that they may speak. He is still able to do these things today, but it is our doubt and unbelief that stop him. When Jesus was on earth, he healed a woman with a blood problem, a man who couldn't walk, and a man who couldn't see. The only difference was that they believed and received. The Lord said that we just need to come to him and he will heal us and make us well from all infirmities no matter what they may be.

*****

Lord, we ask for you to remind us to come to you first concerning our ailments because you are able heal us from sicknesses of all kinds that we may have in our mind, body, and soul.

For insight: Mark 5:8, Matthew 9:35 NIV, Luke 9:11 NIV.

Life's Hidden Challenges

You will tread on the lion and the adder; the young lion and the serpent you will trample underfoot.

Psalm 91:13 NIV

There are struggles and challenges that we face in life that are represented by one of these images: a lion, snake, or a dragon. The lions are bold, and they meet you head-on with unplanned and unexpected things such as death in the family, job loss after years of service, and many others that come into your life. Certain difficulties confront us in life, making us cower or want to flee. The snake strikes, and your heart is filled with fear and terror. Life's unseen wounds, such as betrayal by a friend or family member, are like the stinging attacks of the serpent. The dragons in our lives are the things that we fear may happen, such as being in a plane crash, a car accident, and so on. These fears cause us to fight or flee. We are to fight back using what God has equipped us with, which is his Word and power. It is our relationship with him that is our assurance against these lions, snakes, and dragons of life. Only God is our shelter, to whom we can run when we are being challenged by them.

*****

Lord, we are so thankful that we are not powerless, that you remind us of who we are in you, and that you are our covering.

For insight: Psalm 23:1–6 NKJV,
Isaiah 41:10 NIV.

Grow Your Mustard Seed

If you have faith as small as a mustard seed.

Psalm 17:6 NIV

In walking with the Lord, we start out with what is called a small mustard seed of faith. It's okay to start there, but we can't stay there. The seed is only the beginning, and we need to take our faith to a higher level. The way this is done is through the thunder and lightning of our lives. As we get drenched along the way, it may seem as if we would drown in the unbelief before us because of the situations where it seems impossible for an answer to come. If God does not take us out of the conflict, it is because he has equipped us to win it. During those storms, our faith grows because we can look back and see that the Lord has always made a way through it all.

*****

Lord, you are the one that helps us along the way as our faith grows from a mustard seed and into a strong, tall tree.

For insight: Matthew 13:31–32
KJV, Mark 9:24 NIV.

Watch Your Eye and Ear Gates

Ears that hear and eyes that see, the Lord has made them both.

Proverbs 20:12 NIV

We need to be conscious of what we see and hear on a regular basis. The Lord tells us to be careful of what we allow to go into our eyes and ears because it will enter our hearts. If we are constantly feeding on news media, unending Internet information, and other negative platforms, then it's no wonder that we feel weak, tired, and drained. There is no nourishment for us there; we need to be wise and not overdose ourselves on information that doesn't infuse us with God's life and power. When we are constantly gazing at the wrong things, we will likely flood our minds with the wrong thoughts, which will ultimately affect what we think, feel, say, and do.

Let's choose to stand guard over our hearts by refusing to allow darkness to enter our eyes and ears. The result of being careful of what we allow into those very important gates is that the Lord's Word gives us life and health, which in turn makes us healthier and stronger. We don't want to drown out what is good for us by putting things in us that are not for our well-being.

*****

Lord, we beseech you to assist us in wisely allowing only good things to enter our eye and ear gates so that our hearts may be right before you.

For insight: Proverbs 4:20–22 KJV,
Matthew 13:16 NIV.

Armor Up

Put on the full armor of God, so that you can take your stand against the devil's schemes.

Ephesians 6:11 NIV

The Lord has given us authority, and we are designed to walk fully equipped in the armor that the Lord has given us to wear daily. When we wear the full armor of God, this represents the different parts of our life that we must defend in our spiritual lives. We have been given this suit with all the different parts for our covering. We were not created to be small and cowardly toward the enemies we battle. The Lord wants us to fight with the authority and power he has given us and learn to walk in it day by day. Preparing daily for the battle that is before us. We are to shine in the darkness and walk in victory and in the strength that only comes from God. The armor is truth, righteousness, the Gospel, faith, salvation, God's Word, and prayer. These are the tools we have been given to overcome and be victorious over the attacks and the temptations of our enemy.

*****

Lord, prompt us to remember to put on your armor that covers us in battle. Help us in putting it on daily so that we may be fully dressed and covered for the fight before us.

For insight: Ephesians 6:10–18 NIV,
Isaiah 59:17 NKJV.

Fuel the Fire

"Is not my word like fire," declares the Lord, "and like a hammer that breaks a rock in pieces?"

Jeremiah 23:29 NIV

It takes fuel to have a fire, and it will begin to die down if we do not frequently feed it the materials needed for it to burn powerfully. We ourselves need to regularly fuel our inner fire with the elements needed so that it may also continually burn and not die out. The way we are to do this is by reading the Word of God, which is the fuel we need on a regular basis, and by spending personal time with the Lord. As we do these vital things, we are fueling the inner man, which will continue to burn brightly within us. The Word of God will guide us out of problems, give us insight into matters, and give us direction in the situations we face in our daily lives. We only need to keep his words in our hearts and confess them so that the fire in us burns continuously and brightly.

*****

Lord, we thank you for whenever we read your Word on a daily basis, it fans the fire and makes it burn zealously within us.

For insight: Proverbs 26:21 NKJV,
Jeremiah 20:9 NIV.

Diamond in the Rough

For we are God's handiwork, created in Christ Jesus to do good works, which God prepared in advance for us to do.

Ephesians 2:10 NIV

We are all diamonds in the rough, as the saying goes, and we all have areas in our lives that need to be worked on and polished up. When God finds us, we are often covered with the elements of the world. And just like the diamonds found in the earth, we are rough and uneven and need to be worked on by being cut and polished to bring out the beauty hidden within. The Lord sees each one of us as precious and beautiful, and even though we go through times of pressure and heat in life, it is for our good even though we don't see it that way when we are going through it. The Lord doesn't throw the unfinished diamond aside as someone might throw away a worthless rock because they don't see the beauty within. We are valuable to God, and he sees the potential in us. With a little work, training, and polishing, we will stand out for the Lord and shine brightly for him and for others to see his handiwork.

*****

Lord, we are so grateful that we were hand-picked by you, that you see us as valuable, and that you will also continue to polish us all our lives so that we may continue to shine.

For insight: 1 John 1:9 NKJV,
Philippians 1:6 NIV.

Apple of His Eye

Keep me as the apple of your eye.

Psalm 17:8 NIV

We are very important to God, and he loves us more than we can ever imagine for him to call us the apple of his eye. The Lord keeps his eyes on us and desires for us to keep our eyes on him. There is nothing that escapes the watchful eyes of the Lord because he is always overseeing his creation, including you and me. Just as the light reflects off the shiny skin of an apple, the iris reflects the image of the objects or words that stand before they eye of the beholder. God wants us to keep his words and teachings as the apple of our eyes. If we have not already made this a priority to keep God's Word, then let's begin today by spending some time reading what is of great value to him: the Bible, his written Word.

*****

Lord, remind us to be grateful that you watch over us day and night and that you see us as your people of great worth in your eyes.

For insight: Proverbs 7:2 NIV,
Hebrews 4:13 NIV.

His Treasures

*For where your treasure is, there
your heart will be also.*

Matthew 6:21 NIV

There are many treasures in the Word of God, and to know what they are, we must seek them out so we can find them and attain them. They are abundant throughout the Bible, waiting for us to seek them out. These treasures, such as wisdom and knowledge, has been freely given to us by God. The Lord wants us to have more than enough and beyond measure. Therefore, the more we dig into his word, the more gems we find to add to our spiritual riches of which we will have no lack. Treasures represent what we deem valuable enough to spend one of our most valuable resources on—time.

God's treasures are worth laying in our hearts because they are worth more than anything on this earth. We must be sure of our aim in life: is it to gain riches in this world, or are we aiming toward the riches of the kingdom of God? Because the earthly treasures are temporary, while the heavenly ones last for eternity.

*****

Lord, help us keep looking in your Word for the treasures you've laid out for us to find so that we can grow in you.

For insight: Deuteronomy 7:6 NIV,
2 Corinthians 4:7 NKJV.

Traumas in the Soul

*The Lord is close to the brokenhearted and
saves those who are crushed in spirit.*

Psalm 34:18 NIV

We have all experienced trauma in our lives that we may or may not be aware of. Everyone has experienced adversity at some point in their lives, such as a car accident, job loss, abuse, divorce, death, and so on. What happens in our soul has an impact on our mind, body, and even our physical health. We are all in need of healing in some way; no one is immune to the pains of this world. These traumas also keep us from moving forward in certain areas of our lives because of the emotional and psychological hurt we carry that is unseen to us. God will show us these hidden things if we ask him because he sees them when we cannot. We can then ask the Lord to take these traumas out of our souls by saying this simple prayer as you name the traumas you know you have gone through in life.

Lord, I give you permission to remove every trauma from my soul and heart and make me whole in your precious name, Jesus.

*****

Thank you, Lord, that you free us from the hidden traumas in our soul and that you have touched our minds, bodies, and hearts so that we can now live a life of freedom and joy because we have been set free.

For insight: Isaiah 52:5 NIV,
1 Peter 5:7 NIV

No Room for Anger

Get rid of all bitterness, rage and anger, brawling and slander, along with every form of malice.

Ephesians 4:31 NIV

There are situations in our lives that have happened, and we may have experienced some type of loss, trauma, or even relationships that have failed one way or another and caused us pain that has led us to harbor anger in our hearts. One of the hardest things for us to do in life is to let go of our anger toward ourselves, others, and even God. We do not need to allow anger take hold of us; we have the choice to hold on to it or let it go. If we choose to hold on to our anger, we allow it to take away our peace and joy. We ourselves are powerless to forgive and release the anger we carry unless we have God's strength. Forgiveness is the key to letting go of the hurt and anger and allowing the Lord to fully remove them from our hearts so that we can live our lives with peace, happiness, and contentment.

*****

We want to thank you, Lord, for we can come to you and ask you to remove all anger or resentment from our lives so that we can be fully free and live a life of peace.

For insight: Colossians 3:13 NIV,
James 1:19–20 NIV.

Holy Spirit

Do you not know that your bodies are the temples of the Holy Spirit, who is in you, whom you have received from God? You are not your own.

1 Corinthians 6:19 NIV)

Once we receive the Lord into our lives, God gives to us a helper, who is Holy Spirit. He will teach us all things, guide us in our decisions, and remind us of God's Word that we have read throughout time. The Holy Spirit has been given to us by God so that we can know who he is and also how to follow him and his Word. The Holy Spirit enlightens the Bible and makes the words easier for us to understand, grasp, and apply to our lives. He also gives us insight into the things that God freely gives to us. We are not able to fully appreciate the scriptures if we do not have the Holy Spirit's help because we need him to open up our eyes so we can see the things of God more clearly. He is the one that does that for us. The Holy Spirit is also known as the comforter, and he calms our fears and fills us with hope through the promises God has given to us in his Word.

*****

Lord, we ask for insight into your Word as well as for your Holy Spirit to bring it to our awareness, as we need it as a reminder of what you have said.

For insight: Ephesians 1:13 NKJV,
Romans 8:9 NIV.

My Defense and Shield

You who fear him, trust in the LORD—
he is their help and shield.

Psalm 115:11 NIV)

Our Lord will go before us when we ask for his help and intervention. He will never leave us in defeat. We need to see him as our defender because when we go through trouble, we look at ourselves as defenseless since we forgot to whom we belong. We always exaggerate the problem and make it larger than our God. We must remind ourselves that God is greater than anything we face. If we only stop doing things our way and allow the Lord to be our fortress and shield, he will always take care of the things that concern us when we move out of the way and fully put our trust in him. He will build a fortress around us for our protection against the lies and the schemes of the enemy. He is our shield and buckler in the time of need.

******

We come to you, Lord, and ask you to remind us that you are our defense in times of need, that you are constantly watching over us and keeping us safe.

For insight: Jeremiah 50:31 NIV,
Psalm 18:2 NIV.

It's Time

I have been crucified with Christ and I no longer live, but Christ lives in me.

Galatians 2:20 NIV

Life is a very strenuous and hard thing to do alone, which is why we need the Lord in our lives to keep us on this journey. It is never too late for any of us to come to him or rededicate ourselves; we only need to come to him just as we are. The Lord stands at the door of our hearts and gently knocks, waiting for us to open it so he can enter. The Lord loves you more than you can imagine, and his love is not limited to a single moment as we may love, but it is eternal and never-ending. I would like to invite you at this time to accept him as your personal Lord and savior by saying these few simple words: Lord, I open the door of my heart and ask that you enter and be my savior because I cannot do life on my own. I surrender my life to you and I ask for your help through all the days in my life to walk in your ways. In your precious son's name, Jesus.

*****

You are so loving to us, God, that you wait patiently for us to come to you. You love us so much that the love you have for us is for eternity.

For insight: Romans 10:9–10 NIV,
2 Corinthians 5:17–18 NKJV.

Notes

About the Author

Linda Beltran came from a family of nine children—three boys and six girls, with her being the oldest of the girls. She is a single parent, and she has a son named Angelo that the Lord blessed her with. He is the love of her life—second only to God, of course. She was a teacher for over thirty-seven years, and she loved working with children and adults throughout those years. But God had a different plan for her life, and now here she is—sharing her book of insight, revelation, and inspirational words the Lord impressed upon her to touch others' lives.

These are some of Linda's personal reflections and writings from her quiet times reading the Bible, as well as the journals she has kept throughout the years.

Writing this book has been a process she fought with the Lord for over three years because she kept thinking, "Who am I to do something like that?" The

Lord then showed her that with and through him, anything was possible. He would direct her path and the steps to do what he was leading her to do. So do not ever think that you cannot do something that may seem impossible to you because, with God as your guide, you can do it. Here is her first book, and hopefully, many more will follow.

Be blessed and uplifted!